THE

CLAIRE SWEENEY

BIOGRAPHY

BY

Glenn A. Harris

Table of Contents

CHAPTER 1

Introduction

Overview of Claire Sweeney's Life and Career

Claire Sweeney is a celebrated English actress, singer, television presenter, and theatre performer who has captivated audiences with her diverse talents and charismatic presence. Born on April 17, 1971, in Walton, Liverpool, Claire grew up in a working-class family, which instilled in her a strong sense of determination and resilience. Her journey from humble beginnings to stardom reflects her dedication, versatility, and passion for the performing arts.

Early Aspirations and Training

Claire's interest in entertainment emerged early in life. Encouraged by her family, she pursued training at the prestigious Elliott-Clarke Theatre

School in Liverpool and later attended the Italia Conti Academy of Theatre Arts in London. These institutions provided her with the foundational skills and confidence to excel in acting, singing, and dancing.

Breakthrough Role in Brookside

Claire rose to national prominence in the late 1990s when she joined the cast of Brookside, the groundbreaking British soap opera set in Liverpool. Portraying the character Lindsey Corkhill, Claire won the hearts of viewers with her compelling performance. Her portrayal of Lindsey, a complex and often troubled character, showcased her acting range and established her as a household name. This role became a turning point in her career, earning her widespread recognition and critical acclaim.

Musical Theatre Success

Building on her Brookside success, Claire transitioned to the stage, where she demonstrated her exceptional vocal abilities. She starred in several high-profile West End productions, including Chicago, where she played the iconic role of Roxie Hart, and Guys and Dolls, portraying Miss Adelaide. Her performances were lauded for their energy, charisma, and vocal prowess, solidifying her reputation as a talented musical theatre actress.

Television and Media Career

Claire's charm and versatility made her a popular choice for television roles beyond acting. She became a prominent figure in British entertainment, hosting shows such as 60 Minute Makeover and appearing as a guest on a variety of programs. In 2001, she further endeared herself to the public by participating in the first season of Celebrity Big Brother, where her warm personality and humor shone through.

Music and Recording Career

In addition to her acting and television work, Claire pursued a music career, releasing her debut album, Claire, in 2002. The album featured a mix of show tunes and classic pop standards, showcasing her rich and versatile voice. Her renditions of songs like "Someone to Watch Over Me" were particularly well-received, and the album demonstrated her ability to cross over into the music industry with ease.

Personal Life and Challenges

Throughout her career, Claire has been open about her personal life, including her relationships and her journey as a mother. In 2014, she welcomed her son, Jaxon, who became a central figure in her life. Despite the challenges of balancing a demanding career with motherhood, Claire has continued to thrive professionally and remains a beloved figure in British entertainment.

Philanthropy and Advocacy

Beyond her professional achievements, Claire is deeply committed to philanthropy. She has supported numerous charitable causes, including those focused on children, health, and the arts. Her efforts have further endeared her to the public, demonstrating her generosity and compassion.

Continued Relevance and Legacy

Claire Sweeney's career has spanned over three decades, during which she has continuously reinvented herself. Whether on stage, screen, or in the recording studio, she has remained a versatile and engaging performer. Her ability to connect with audiences across different mediums highlights her enduring appeal and impact on the entertainment industry.

Purpose of the Biography

The purpose of this biography is to provide a comprehensive and insightful account of Claire Sweeney's life, career, and contributions to the entertainment industry. It seeks to explore her journey from humble beginnings in Liverpool to becoming a celebrated actress, singer, and television personality, highlighting the determination, talent, and resilience that have defined her career.

This biography aims to:

1. Inspire Aspiring Performers

By detailing Claire's rise to prominence, the challenges she faced, and the achievements she attained, this biography serves as an inspirational story for those pursuing careers in the performing arts. Her journey exemplifies the importance of hard work, dedication, and adaptability in achieving success.

2. Celebrate Her Contributions to the Arts

Claire Sweeney's impact on television, theatre, and music is significant. The biography chronicles her major roles, performances, and projects, showcasing her versatility and influence in the British entertainment industry.

3. Provide a Personal Insight

Beyond her professional life, this biography delves into Claire's personal experiences, including her relationships, motherhood, and philanthropic endeavors. This humanizes her story, offering readers a deeper understanding of the person behind the public persona.

4. Document Cultural Influence

Claire's work reflects broader trends in British entertainment and culture over the past three decades. The biography examines how her roles and public image have contributed to shaping popular culture, particularly in the realms of television and musical theatre.

5. Preserve Her Legacy

As an enduring figure in the entertainment industry, Claire Sweeney's life story is worth documenting for future generations. This biography ensures her achievements and contributions are recognized and remembered as part of the cultural and artistic history of the United Kingdom.

CHAPTER 2

Early Life
Childhood and Family Background

Claire Sweeney was born on April 17, 1971, in Walton, Liverpool, England, into a working-class family that provided her with a supportive and loving foundation. She was the eldest child of Ken Sweeney, a mechanic, and Kathleen Sweeney, a cashier. Growing up in a close-knit community, Claire was deeply influenced by the warmth and resilience of her family, values that would shape her approach to life and career.

A Childhood in Liverpool

Claire's childhood was rooted in the vibrant culture of Liverpool, a city renowned for its strong ties to music, art, and theatre. This environment played a pivotal role in sparking her early interest in performing arts. Despite financial challenges, her parents ensured she had access to opportunities that nurtured her creativity and ambition.

Discovering a Passion for Performing

From a young age, Claire displayed a natural talent for entertaining. She often participated in school plays and local events, where her energetic performances caught the attention of teachers and neighbors. Encouraged by her family, she began attending dance classes and local performing arts programs, which allowed her to refine her skills in acting and singing.

Early Challenges and Determination

Life was not without its difficulties. Growing up in a working-class household meant resources were often limited, but Claire's determination and the unwavering support of her parents helped her overcome these challenges. Her father, in particular, encouraged her to pursue her dreams, teaching her the value of hard work and perseverance.

Support from Her Community

The Liverpool community also played a crucial role in Claire's upbringing. Surrounded by a culture of storytelling and music, she absorbed the artistic energy of her environment, which would later influence her career in musical theatre and television.

Education and Training Foundations

Recognizing her potential, her parents enrolled her in the Elliott-Clarke Theatre School in Liverpool, where she received formal training in dance, acting, and singing. This marked the beginning of her professional journey in the arts. Later, Claire won a scholarship to the Italia Conti Academy of Theatre Arts in London, further honing her skills and preparing her for a successful career.

A Family-Oriented Upbringing

Despite her growing ambitions, Claire remained deeply connected to her family. Her upbringing instilled in her a strong sense of loyalty and gratitude, traits that she has carried throughout her life. She often credits her family's support and sacrifices as the foundation of her success.

Education and Early Influences

Claire Sweeney's education and early influences played a pivotal role in shaping her career as a multi-talented performer. Her passion for the performing arts became evident from an early age, and with the support of her family and community, she pursued her dreams with determination.

Early Schooling and Introduction to the Arts

Claire attended primary school in her hometown of Liverpool, where she was an active participant in school plays and performances. Her natural flair for acting and singing stood out, earning her praise from teachers and classmates. These early experiences ignited her passion for entertaining and set her on a path toward a career in the arts.

Elliott-Clarke Theatre School

Recognizing her potential, Claire's parents enrolled her in the prestigious Elliott-Clarke Theatre School in Liverpool. This institution, known for nurturing creative talent, provided her with foundational training in acting, singing, and dancing. It was here that Claire began to develop the technical skills and confidence required to perform on stage and screen.

At Elliott-Clarke, Claire was exposed to a wide range of artistic disciplines, including classical theatre, musical performance, and modern dance. The school's rigorous curriculum and emphasis on professionalism helped her understand the demands of the entertainment industry, preparing her for the challenges ahead.

Early Influences

During her formative years, Claire drew inspiration from several sources:

Liverpool's Rich Cultural Scene: Growing up in Liverpool, a city renowned for its contributions to music, theatre, and art, Claire was surrounded by creativity. The city's cultural vibrancy, particularly its ties to iconic performers like The Beatles, inspired her to dream big.

Family Support: Her parents, especially her father, were instrumental in encouraging her to pursue a career in the arts. Their belief in her abilities gave her the confidence to explore her talents.

Performing Arts Icons: Claire admired performers who excelled in multiple disciplines, such as Barbra Streisand and Liza Minnelli, and aspired to emulate their versatility and charisma.

Italia Conti Academy of Theatre Arts

Claire's journey continued when she earned a scholarship to the Italia Conti Academy of Theatre Arts in London, one of the UK's most renowned performing arts schools. This marked a significant milestone in her life, as it allowed her to refine her craft and gain exposure to industry professionals.

At Italia Conti, Claire honed her skills in acting, vocal performance, and dance. The academy also emphasized discipline and resilience, qualities that would prove invaluable throughout her career. During her time there, she performed in student productions, showcasing her talent and building connections that would later help launch her professional career.

Early Professional Experiences

While studying, Claire began taking small jobs to support herself, including singing in local pubs and clubs. These early gigs not only helped her financially but also allowed her to gain practical experience in performing for live audiences. It was during these years that she developed her stage presence and learned how to connect with her audience, a skill that would become one of her trademarks.

Shaping Her Ambitions

The combination of formal education, practical experience, and a supportive network of mentors and family shaped Claire's ambitions and gave her a clear vision of her future. By the time she graduated from Italia Conti, she was well-equipped to embark on a career in entertainment.

CHAPTER 3

Rise to Fame

Breakthrough in Television

Claire Sweeney's breakthrough in television came with her role as Lindsey Corkhill in the iconic British soap opera Brookside. This opportunity marked a turning point in her career, catapulting her into the spotlight and establishing her as a household name in the UK entertainment industry.

Joining Brookside

In 1991, Claire joined the cast of Brookside, a groundbreaking Channel 4 soap opera set in Liverpool. Created by Phil Redmond, the show was known for tackling controversial and socially relevant issues. Claire portrayed Lindsey Corkhill, a member of one of the show's most infamous families, the Corkhills. Lindsey was a complex character, often caught in a web of dramatic storylines involving love, crime, and family conflict.

Making an Impact

Claire's performance as Lindsey Corkhill resonated deeply with audiences. She brought depth and nuance to the role, skillfully portraying Lindsey's struggles and resilience. Her natural charisma and emotional range helped make the character relatable and memorable, earning her widespread acclaim.

One of her most notable storylines involved Lindsey's tumultuous relationship with her husband, which explored themes of loyalty, betrayal, and redemption. These gripping narratives not only captivated viewers but also showcased Claire's acting versatility.

Leaving and Returning

Claire left Brookside in 1993 to explore other opportunities but returned in 1995 due to popular demand. Her comeback brought renewed energy to the show, and she remained a central figure until her final departure in 2001. This role solidified her reputation as one of the most talented actresses of her generation.

Recognition and Popularity

During her time on Brookside, Claire became one of the most recognizable faces on British television. Her portrayal of Lindsey Corkhill earned her critical praise and a loyal fan base. The role not only boosted her career but also opened doors to other opportunities in the entertainment industry, including theatre and presenting roles.

Lasting Legacy

Brookside remains a defining chapter in Claire Sweeney's career. The show's bold storytelling and Claire's standout performance as Lindsey Corkhill left a lasting impression on British television history. The experience also provided Claire with a platform to transition into other areas of entertainment, demonstrating her versatility as a performer.

Beyond Brookside

After her departure from the show, Claire used the skills and recognition she gained to take on diverse roles across television, stage, and music. Her time on Brookside served as the foundation for her successful career in the entertainment industry.

Role on Brookside and Its Impact

Claire Sweeney's portrayal of Lindsey Corkhill on the British soap opera Brookside remains one of the most significant roles of her career. Her work on the show not only brought her national recognition but also cemented her status as a versatile and talented actress. The character of Lindsey Corkhill, and Claire's performance in the role, had a lasting impact on the show's legacy and the broader British television landscape.

The Role of Lindsey Corkhill

Claire joined Brookside in 1991, playing Lindsey Corkhill, a member of the notorious Corkhill family. Lindsey was a compelling and multi-dimensional character whose storylines explored a wide range of emotional and social issues. She was portrayed as a strong-willed yet vulnerable woman navigating the challenges of life, relationships, and family drama.

Key aspects of Lindsey Corkhill's character included:

Family Dynamics: As the daughter of Jimmy and Jackie Corkhill, Lindsey's relationships with her family were central to many of the show's storylines. These dynamics highlighted themes of loyalty, betrayal, and forgiveness.

Romantic Relationships: Lindsey's tumultuous marriage and relationships showcased Claire's ability to handle complex emotional material, adding depth to her character.

Moral Complexity: Lindsey often found herself entangled in morally ambiguous situations, including criminal activities, which added layers to her character and kept viewers intrigued.

Claire's Performance

Claire's portrayal of Lindsey Corkhill stood out for its authenticity and emotional intensity. She brought depth and humanity to the character, making Lindsey relatable and sympathetic despite her flaws. Claire's natural charisma and emotional range resonated with audiences, helping to make Lindsey one of the show's most memorable characters.

Notable Storylines

Lindsey Corkhill was at the center of several iconic Brookside storylines, including:

Domestic Struggles: Her marriage was fraught with challenges, including infidelity and financial problems, reflecting real-life issues faced by many viewers.

Crime and Redemption: Lindsey's involvement in criminal activities, such as money laundering, added intrigue and drama to the show while exploring themes of morality and consequence.

Empowerment and Independence: Over time, Lindsey evolved into a stronger, more independent character, earning the admiration of fans who saw her as a survivor.

Impact on Brookside

Lindsey Corkhill became a central figure in Brookside, and her storylines were instrumental in maintaining the show's popularity during its run. Claire's performance contributed significantly to the show's reputation for tackling complex, socially relevant issues.

The Corkhill family, in particular, became emblematic of Brookside's ability to depict the struggles of working-class families with authenticity and depth. Lindsey's character added a human element to the family's often chaotic storylines, making her a fan favorite.

Impact on Claire Sweeney's Career

Playing Lindsey Corkhill was a breakthrough for Claire Sweeney. The role brought her widespread acclaim and established her as a household name in the UK. It also showcased her acting versatility, leading to opportunities in other areas of entertainment, including musical theatre and presenting.

Cultural Legacy

Claire's role on Brookside remains an enduring part of British television history. The show itself is remembered for its bold storytelling and willingness to address controversial topics, and Lindsey Corkhill's character played a significant role in this legacy. For many fans, Claire Sweeney's performance continues to be synonymous with the show's golden years.

CHAPTER 4

Stage Career
Musical Theatre Roles

Claire Sweeney has enjoyed a successful career in musical theatre, showcasing her exceptional talent as a singer, actress, and dancer. Her performances in various acclaimed productions have earned her widespread recognition and cemented her status as a versatile and accomplished performer. Below is an overview of some of her most notable roles in musical theatre.

1. Chicago (2001–2002)

Role: Roxie Hart

Production: West End

Overview:

Claire's portrayal of Roxie Hart in Chicago marked a significant milestone in her theatre career. As the ambitious and cunning showgirl who dreams of stardom, Claire brought charm, wit, and a captivating stage presence to the role. Her performance, which included iconic numbers such as "Roxie" and "Funny Honey," received critical acclaim. She proved her versatility by seamlessly transitioning from television to a demanding musical theatre role.

Impact:

The role of Roxie Hart showcased Claire's ability to take on a leading role in a major West End production. It solidified her reputation as a formidable talent in musical theatre.

2. Guys and Dolls (2005)

Role: Miss Adelaide

Production: UK Tour

Overview:

Claire played the role of Miss Adelaide, a lovable and comically frustrated nightclub singer and fiancée of Nathan Detroit. Her performance in Guys and Dolls highlighted her comedic timing and vocal range, particularly in songs like "Adelaide's Lament." The character's blend of humor and vulnerability allowed Claire to demonstrate her acting depth and endear herself to audiences.

Impact:

This role further established Claire's credentials as a leading lady in musical theatre and demonstrated her ability to handle both comedic and dramatic material.

3. Tell Me on a Sunday (2004)

Role: Solo Performer

Production: UK Tour

Overview:

In this one-woman musical by Andrew Lloyd Webber, Claire delivered a powerful performance that chronicled the journey of a British woman navigating love and life in New York City. The intimate setting and emotional depth of the show allowed Claire to connect deeply with her audience, showcasing her ability to carry an entire production on her own.

Impact:

Her performance was praised for its emotional authenticity and vocal strength, reaffirming her status as a versatile and compelling performer.

4. Fosse (2000)

Role: Featured Performer

Production: West End

Overview:

Claire joined the cast of Fosse, a tribute to legendary choreographer Bob Fosse, where she demonstrated her skills in dance and performance. The production, known for its demanding choreography and sultry style, allowed Claire to showcase her versatility and adaptability as a performer.

Impact:

This experience further refined her stage presence and ability to meet the physical demands of musical theatre.

5. White Christmas (2009)

Role: Betty Haynes

Production: UK Tour

Overview:

In this festive musical adaptation of the classic film White Christmas, Claire played Betty Haynes, a singer in a sister act. Her performance captured the elegance and warmth of the character, with standout moments in songs like "Sisters" and "Love, You Didn't Do Right by Me."

Impact:

This role highlighted Claire's ability to perform in nostalgic, family-friendly productions while maintaining her signature charisma and vocal excellence.

6. 9 to 5: The Musical (2012)

Role: Violet Newstead

Production: UK Tour

Overview:

Claire took on the role of Violet Newstead, a smart and determined office worker seeking justice in a male-dominated workplace. The role required strong comedic timing and a commanding stage presence, both of which Claire delivered effortlessly.

Impact:

Her portrayal resonated with audiences and critics alike, showcasing her ability to balance humor and empowerment in a musical role.

7. Chitty Chitty Bang Bang (2016)

Role: Baroness Bomburst

Production: UK Tour

Overview:

As the flamboyant and eccentric Baroness Bomburst, Claire embraced a comedic and villainous role in this family-friendly musical. Her exaggerated antics and humorous delivery made her performance a standout in the production.

Impact:

This role demonstrated Claire's willingness to explore diverse character types and her ability to excel in larger-than-life roles.

Overall Impact on Career

Claire Sweeney's musical theatre roles have been instrumental in showcasing her versatility as a performer. Her ability to inhabit a wide range of characters from comedic to dramatic, glamorous to down-to-earth has solidified her reputation as one of the UK's most accomplished stage performers.

Notable Performances in the West End

Claire Sweeney has delivered a series of remarkable performances in London's West End, cementing her status as one of the most versatile and charismatic performers in British theatre. Her roles in iconic productions have showcased her talents in acting, singing, and dancing, making her a beloved figure on the West End stage.

1. Chicago (2001–2002)

Role: Roxie Hart

Overview:

Claire's debut as Roxie Hart in the musical Chicago was a defining moment in her West End career. As the ambitious and scheming showgirl, she brought a perfect mix of wit, charm, and vulnerability to the role. Her performance of the iconic songs "Roxie" and "Funny Honey" captivated audiences and earned her critical acclaim.

Highlights:

Claire's ability to embody Roxie's blend of naivety and cunning made her portrayal particularly memorable.

Her dance sequences, choreographed in Bob Fosse's signature style, showcased her physical agility and stage presence.

Impact:

This role not only established her as a leading lady in musical theatre but also proved her ability to transition seamlessly from television to the stage.

2. Fosse (2000)

Role: Featured Performer

Overview:

In this tribute to the legendary choreographer Bob Fosse, Claire demonstrated her prowess as a dancer and performer. The production featured Fosse's iconic choreography, requiring precision, grace, and a deep understanding of his unique style.

Highlights:

Claire excelled in delivering the sultry and dynamic movements characteristic of Fosse's choreography.

Her performance was noted for its elegance and energy, contributing to the overall success of the production.

Impact:

This role helped Claire gain recognition as a versatile performer capable of excelling in demanding musical theatre productions.

3. Tell Me on a Sunday (2004)

Role: Solo Performer

Overview:

Claire took on the challenging role of a solo performer in Andrew Lloyd Webber's Tell Me on a Sunday. This one-act musical follows the emotional journey of an English woman navigating love and heartbreak in New York City.

Highlights:

Claire's powerful rendition of the title song, "Tell Me on a Sunday," was a standout moment in the production.

Her ability to convey a wide range of emotions, from hope to despair, made her performance deeply moving and relatable.

Impact:

The role showcased Claire's vocal strength and acting depth, proving her ability to carry an entire production on her own.

4. Legally Blonde (2011)

Role: Paulette Bonafonté

Overview:

In this adaptation of the hit film, Claire played Paulette, the lovable and comedic hairdresser. Her performance brought warmth and humor to the role, delighting audiences with her charm and impeccable comedic timing.

Highlights:

Her performance of "Ireland," a comedic yet heartfelt number, became an audience favorite.

Claire's interactions with other characters added layers of humor and relatability to the production.

Impact:

This role demonstrated Claire's ability to excel in comedic roles and solidified her reputation as a versatile actress.

5. Hairspray (2012)

Role: Velma Von Tussle

Overview:

Claire played the antagonistic Velma Von Tussle, the snobbish and manipulative producer of The Corny Collins Show. Her portrayal balanced humor and villainy, making Velma a captivating and entertaining character.

Highlights:

Her commanding stage presence brought an edge to the role, making Velma both glamorous and formidable.

Claire's vocal performance in numbers like "Miss Baltimore Crabs" was widely praised.

Impact:

The role allowed Claire to showcase her ability to take on larger-than-life characters and deliver standout performances.

Legacy in the West End

Claire Sweeney's notable West End performances reflect her adaptability and talent across a wide range of roles. From sultry and ambitious characters like Roxie Hart in Chicago to comedic and heartfelt roles like Paulette in Legally Blonde, she has consistently impressed audiences and critics alike. Her ability to seamlessly blend acting, singing, and dancing has made her a celebrated figure in the world of musical theatre.

CHAPTER 5

Television and Media Presence
Hosting Roles and TV Appearances

Claire Sweeney's career extends beyond acting and musical theatre into television presenting and hosting. Her natural charisma, wit, and relatable personality have made her a popular choice for a variety of TV programs, from entertainment shows to lifestyle features. Below is a detailed look at her hosting roles and notable TV appearances.

1. 60 Minute Makeover (2011–2012)

Role: Host

Overview:

Claire hosted the popular ITV home improvement series 60 Minute Makeover, where a team of experts transformed homes within an hour. Her warm and engaging style resonated with viewers, making her a standout host.

Highlights:

Claire's ability to connect with homeowners added a personal touch to the show.

Her enthusiasm and energy helped maintain the fast-paced and uplifting tone of the program.

Impact:

This role showcased her versatility as a television presenter and expanded her appeal to lifestyle and home renovation audiences.

2. Loose Women (Guest Presenter and Panelist)

Role: Regular Guest and Occasional Host

Overview:

Claire has appeared as a guest presenter and panelist on ITV's daytime talk show Loose Women. Known for its candid discussions on current events, relationships, and lifestyle topics, the show allowed Claire to share her perspectives and humor with viewers.

Highlights:

Claire's openness and quick wit made her a natural fit for the show.

Her anecdotes and insights about her career and personal life endeared her to audiences.

Impact:

Her appearances on Loose Women reinforced her image as a relatable and multi-talented entertainer.

3. Here Comes the Sun (2006)

Role: Co-Host

Overview:

Claire co-hosted this ITV travel and lifestyle show, which explored holiday destinations and leisure activities. Her role involved presenting segments on luxurious getaways and family-friendly travel spots.

Highlights:

Claire's engaging on-screen presence brought vibrancy to the show.

Her ability to convey genuine enthusiasm for travel destinations made her segments particularly appealing.

Impact:

The program allowed Claire to branch out into lifestyle and travel television, showcasing her adaptability as a presenter.

4. Celebrity Big Brother (2001)

Role: Contestant (2nd Place)

Overview:

Claire participated in the first-ever UK season of Celebrity Big Brother. Her genuine and down-to-earth personality won over viewers, earning her the runner-up position.

Highlights:

Claire's humor and ability to connect with her fellow contestants made her a standout participant.

Her appearance helped increase her popularity with a broader audience.

Impact:

This experience boosted Claire's profile and paved the way for future television opportunities.

5. The Claire Sweeney Show (2004)

Role: Host

Overview:

Claire hosted her own variety show on ITV, which featured celebrity interviews, comedy sketches, and musical performances. The program allowed Claire to combine her hosting skills with her love for music and entertainment.

Highlights:

Her interviews with high-profile guests showcased her skills as a conversationalist.

Her musical numbers added a unique and personal touch to the show.

Impact:

The show highlighted Claire's ability to lead a prime-time entertainment program, solidifying her status as a versatile performer.

6. Strictly Come Dancing: It Takes Two (Guest)

Role: Guest Commentator

Overview:

As a guest on the companion show to BBC's Strictly Come Dancing, Claire provided commentary and insights about the contestants and their performances.

Highlights:

Claire's background in musical theatre allowed her to offer expert opinions on the technical aspects of dance.

Her lively and engaging commentary was well-received by fans of the show.

7. Saturday Night Live with Claire Sweeney (2002)

Role: Host

Overview:

Claire hosted this one-off Saturday night entertainment special on ITV, showcasing her charm and versatility as a presenter. The program featured musical performances, comedy skits, and audience interaction.

Other Notable TV Appearances

Acting Roles: Claire has appeared in several guest roles on TV dramas, including Doctors and Benidorm.

Documentaries: She has also featured in personal documentaries such as Claire Sweeney: My Big Fat Diet (2008), where she explored diet and fitness challenges, reflecting her willingness to address relatable issues.

Legacy as a TV Personality

Claire Sweeney's work in television reflects her ability to connect with audiences across various formats, from reality TV and lifestyle programs to talk shows and entertainment specials. Her charisma, relatability, and professionalism have made her a beloved figure on British television, complementing her accomplishments in acting and musical theatre.

Participation in Reality Shows

Claire Sweeney's involvement in reality television has been a notable aspect of her career, showcasing her relatable personality, humor, and willingness to embrace new challenges. Her appearances have ranged from competitive formats to lifestyle explorations, allowing audiences to see her in a more personal and unfiltered light. Below is a detailed look at her participation in reality shows.

1. Celebrity Big Brother (2001)

Role: Contestant (Runner-Up)

Overview:

Claire was one of the inaugural participants in the first-ever UK season of Celebrity Big Brother. Her down-to-earth demeanor, sense of humor, and ability to get along with fellow housemates made her a fan favorite. She ultimately finished as the runner-up.

Highlights:

Claire formed genuine connections with other contestants, showcasing her approachable and friendly nature.

Her candid and relatable moments, including discussions about her career and personal life, resonated with viewers.

Impact:

Claire's participation in Celebrity Big Brother increased her public profile significantly and introduced her to a broader audience. It also demonstrated her willingness to step out of her comfort zone and engage with fans in an unfiltered environment.

2. Strictly Come Dancing (2004)

Role: Contestant

Overview:

Claire competed in the second series of BBC's Strictly Come Dancing, partnering with professional dancer John Byrnes. As a trained performer, Claire's participation brought elegance and flair to the dance floor.

Highlights:

Claire impressed the judges and audience with her natural rhythm and ability to master complex routines.

Her performance of ballroom and Latin dances, including the foxtrot and cha-cha, showcased her versatility.

Impact:

Though she did not win, Claire's appearance further cemented her reputation as a multi-talented entertainer. It also introduced her to fans of dance and live performance.

3. Claire Sweeney: My Big Fat Diet (2008)

Role: Participant and Subject

Overview:

This ITV documentary followed Claire as she explored the challenges of diet and fitness. She temporarily abandoned her healthy lifestyle to understand the effects of an unhealthy diet on her body and mind.

Highlights:

Claire's candid and vulnerable approach to discussing body image and health issues made the show relatable and insightful.

The documentary featured Claire undergoing medical tests and personal challenges, offering an honest look at the struggles many people face with diet and weight management.

Impact:

The program was well-received for its educational value and Claire's openness, highlighting her ability to engage with serious topics in an accessible way.

4. Celebrity Hunted (2021)

Role: Contestant

Overview:

Claire participated in the reality show Celebrity Hunted, where celebrities attempt to evade capture by a team of professional hunters. Claire's ingenuity and resourcefulness were on full display as she navigated the challenges of staying off the grid.

Highlights:

Her humorous and relatable moments, combined with her determination, made her a standout contestant.

The show highlighted her adventurous spirit and willingness to embrace new challenges.

Impact:

Claire's participation demonstrated her adaptability and courage, endearing her to fans who appreciated her efforts in an unfamiliar and high-pressure environment.

5. Celebs on the Farm (2019)

Role: Contestant

Overview:

Claire joined this reality show where celebrities took on the challenge of living and working on a farm. From herding animals to performing manual labor, Claire embraced the rural lifestyle with enthusiasm and humor.

Highlights:

Claire's willingness to tackle farm-related tasks, often with comedic results, made her a favorite on the show.

Her interactions with other contestants revealed her collaborative and fun-loving nature.

Impact:

This appearance showcased her ability to adapt to unfamiliar environments and reinforced her reputation as a versatile and down-to-earth celebrity.

6. The Real Full Monty (2018)

Role: Participant

Overview:

Claire took part in The Real Full Monty, a reality show where celebrities perform a choreographed striptease to raise awareness for cancer charities. The show tackled serious issues with a mix of humor and heart.

Highlights:

Claire's performance was both empowering and entertaining, emphasizing body positivity and confidence.

Her dedication to supporting a meaningful cause resonated with viewers.

Impact:

The program demonstrated Claire's willingness to use her platform for advocacy and her courage to participate in a bold and emotionally charged project.

Legacy in Reality Television

Claire Sweeney's participation in reality shows has highlighted her multi-faceted personality, blending charm, humor, and relatability. Whether competing, advocating for important causes, or exploring lifestyle challenges, Claire's authenticity and approachability have consistently resonated with audiences. These appearances have not only expanded her fan base but also showcased her versatility beyond acting and theatre.

CHAPTER 6

Music Career

Album Releases and Chart Success

Claire Sweeney's foray into music has added another dimension to her entertainment career.

While she is best known for her acting and television work, she has also released music albums that showcase her vocal talent and musical versatility. Below is a look at her album releases and chart success.

1. Claire Sweeney (2000)

Album Overview:

In 2000, Claire Sweeney released her debut album simply titled Claire Sweeney. The album featured a mix of pop and musical theatre standards, displaying her vocal range and her ability to transition between genres.

Tracks and Highlights:

The album included tracks such as "I Don't Know How to Love Him" (from Jesus Christ Superstar) and "The Greatest Love of All."

Claire's voice was praised for its clarity and emotional delivery, particularly on the ballads.

Chart Success:

While the album did not make a major impact on the UK charts, it earned a dedicated fan following and helped establish Claire as a musical performer.

The album's release was supported by various media appearances, allowing Claire to showcase her singing talent to a wider audience.

Impact:

Claire's debut album helped solidify her position as a multi-talented entertainer, drawing attention to her ability to combine musical theatre with pop sensibilities.

2. Sweeney's Songs (2005)

Album Overview:

In 2005, Claire released Sweeney's Songs, an album that continued her exploration of the musical theatre genre, as well as her passion for pop and contemporary music. The album included a blend of well-known songs from stage productions and original tracks.

Tracks and Highlights:

The album featured tracks like "Somewhere Over the Rainbow" and "I Know Him So Well," showcasing Claire's classical vocal training and her ability to handle a variety of musical styles.

Claire also included original songs, adding a more personal touch to the album.

Chart Success:

Sweeney's Songs did not achieve major chart success but gained popularity among musical theatre fans and those who appreciated Claire's work on stage.

It was well-received in terms of performance and style, with some tracks making it onto smaller, niche charts within the musical theatre scene.

Impact:

This album further solidified Claire as a performer with a unique blend of musical theatre and pop influences. It appealed to fans who were drawn to her stage performances and showcased her as an established recording artist.

3. The Christmas Album (2011)

Album Overview:

In 2011, Claire Sweeney released a festive album titled The Christmas Album, which featured a collection of classic holiday songs performed in her signature style. The album's release added a seasonal touch to her musical repertoire, appealing to fans of both traditional and contemporary Christmas music.

Tracks and Highlights:

The album included timeless holiday favorites like "Silent Night," "White Christmas," and "Have Yourself a Merry Little Christmas."

Claire's renditions of these classic songs were praised for their warmth and emotional depth, capturing the spirit of the season.

Chart Success:

The album performed modestly on the UK charts, with several tracks being featured on Christmas-themed playlists and compilations.

It resonated well with listeners looking for a fresh, yet nostalgic take on Christmas music.

Impact:

The Christmas Album allowed Claire to expand her musical portfolio while tapping into the popular holiday music market. It provided a refreshing and festive alternative to traditional Christmas music albums.

Chart Performance and Reception

Although Claire Sweeney's albums did not achieve major commercial chart success, they garnered a loyal fan base and received positive reviews for her vocal abilities and the variety of songs featured. Her albums typically catered to fans of musical theatre and those interested in her work as a performer. The combination of theatrical songs and contemporary tracks demonstrated her range and passion for music, further enhancing her reputation as a multi-talented artist.

Legacy in Music

Claire Sweeney's contributions to the music industry may not have been dominated by chart-topping hits, but they were instrumental in showcasing her as a well-rounded entertainer. Her music albums revealed her deep connection to the world of musical theatre while allowing her to experiment with different styles. For fans of musical theatre, her vocal performances have been highly regarded, with her albums continuing to reflect her passion for both the stage and the recording studio.

Notable Songs and Performances

Claire Sweeney has showcased her vocal talent through various notable songs and performances across both her music albums and live shows. Her work spans from musical theatre classics to contemporary pop and festive tunes, allowing her to display a versatile and captivating voice. Below is a detailed look at some of her most notable songs and live performances.

1. "I Don't Know How to Love Him" (from Jesus Christ Superstar)

Performance Overview:

One of the standout songs from Claire's musical theatre repertoire, Claire performed "I Don't Know How to Love Him" from the iconic rock opera Jesus Christ Superstar. The song is a heartfelt ballad sung by Mary Magdalene, reflecting her emotional struggle in love and devotion.

Notable Performance:

Claire performed this song as part of her debut album Claire Sweeney (2000) and in her stage performances, where her emotional delivery captured the complexity of the character's feelings.

Impact:

This ballad demonstrated Claire's vocal range and emotional depth, which helped cement her reputation as a skilled singer capable of tackling both contemporary and classic musical theatre pieces.

2. "Somewhere Over the Rainbow"

Performance Overview:

One of the most iconic songs in musical theatre, "Somewhere Over the Rainbow" from The Wizard of Oz has been performed by countless artists. Claire's rendition of this timeless classic was featured on her second album Sweeney's Songs (2005).

Notable Performance:

Her version of the song was marked by its purity and emotion, with Claire's voice soaring through the famous melody. She brought a fresh, heartfelt interpretation to this beloved standard.

Impact:

Claire's interpretation of this song became one of her signature performances, highlighting her ability to infuse well-known songs with her own unique style and emotional intensity.

3. "The Greatest Love of All"

Performance Overview:

Originally performed by Whitney Houston, "The Greatest Love of All" is a powerful anthem about self-respect and empowerment. Claire's version was featured on her debut album Claire Sweeney (2000).

Notable Performance:

Claire's rendition was characterized by its emotional strength and vocal control, and she managed to make it her own while still honoring the original version.

Impact:

The performance demonstrated Claire's vocal power and her ability to tackle strong, emotional ballads, further establishing her as a versatile performer across different musical genres.

4. "I Know Him So Well" (from Chess)

Performance Overview:

"I Know Him So Well," a duet from the musical Chess, became one of the most iconic songs of musical theatre. Claire performed it with fellow actress Rachel Tucker as part of Sweeney's Songs (2005).

Notable Performance:

This performance showcased Claire's vocal harmony with Tucker, as both singers blended their voices beautifully. The song's theme of unspoken love and mutual understanding was captured in their compelling performance.

Impact:

The performance of "I Know Him So Well" received acclaim for its vocal precision and chemistry, proving Claire's ability to perform both solo and in collaboration with other artists

5. "Silent Night"

Performance Overview:

"Silent Night," the beloved Christmas carol, was featured on Claire's Christmas Album (2011). This serene and moving song was a perfect fit for her warm vocal tone.

Notable Performance:

Claire's rendition of "Silent Night" was praised for its emotional depth, bringing a sense of calm and reverence to the song. The arrangement was simple, allowing her voice to shine without unnecessary embellishments.

Impact:

Her performance of "Silent Night" is widely remembered as one of the highlights of her Christmas album, showcasing her ability to evoke deep emotion through familiar seasonal songs.

6. "Have Yourself a Merry Little Christmas"

Performance Overview:

Another holiday classic featured on Claire's Christmas Album (2011), "Have Yourself a Merry Little Christmas" has been covered by countless artists over the years. Claire's version captured the nostalgic and sentimental qualities of the song.

Notable Performance:

Claire's delivery was heartfelt, with a warmth that made the song both intimate and festive. Her vocal performance made this classic her own, particularly in its rich, sincere tone.

Impact:

This song's success highlighted Claire's ability to perform holiday tunes with emotional resonance, making her Christmas album a memorable and enjoyable listen for fans.

7. "Miss Baltimore Crabs" (from Hairspray)

Performance Overview:

In her role as Velma Von Tussle in the West End production of Hairspray (2012), Claire performed "Miss Baltimore Crabs," a cheeky and high-energy number that highlighted her comedic timing and vocal abilities.

Notable Performance:

Her portrayal of Velma was a blend of humor, arrogance, and theatrical flair, with Claire delivering the song with sharp wit and impressive vocal control.

Impact:

This performance became one of Claire's most celebrated, as it showcased her ability to play a villainous character with humor and sass, all while delivering a show-stopping musical number.

Legacy of Claire Sweeney's Songs and Performances

Claire Sweeney's songs and performances have left a lasting impact in both the musical theatre and music industries. Whether performing powerful ballads, such as "Somewhere Over the Rainbow," or taking on the sass and energy of "Miss Baltimore Crabs," Claire's vocal versatility has been a key factor in her success. Her performances across a range of musical styles demonstrate her ability to adapt to various genres, ensuring her place as a well-respected performer both on stage and in the recording studio.

CHAPTER 7

Personal Life
Relationships and Family

Claire Sweeney's personal life, particularly her relationships and family, has been an important aspect of her public persona. Over the years, she has been open about her experiences and values, especially regarding her role as a mother and her past relationships. Below is a detailed look at Claire's relationships and family life.

Early Relationships and Public Life

Before becoming a mother, Claire had several high-profile relationships, many of which were covered by the media. As a public figure, she often found her personal life subject to attention, which she navigated with grace and openness.

Engagement to Daniel Reilly (2004)

In 2004, Claire became engaged to businessman Daniel Reilly. The couple's engagement attracted considerable media interest, but they eventually parted ways. While the relationship ended, Claire has spoken positively about the experience, indicating that it was a significant part of her life at the time.

Motherhood: Birth of Her Son

One of the most pivotal moments in Claire Sweeney's life was becoming a mother. Claire's relationship with her son, named Billy, has been central to her happiness and personal growth.

Son's Birth (2011)

In 2011, Claire gave birth to her son Billy, whom she shares with her ex-partner, former actor and television producer David Love. Becoming a mother marked a new chapter in her life, and she has since spoken about the joy and challenges of parenthood.

Claire was initially cautious about revealing details about her private life but later became more open, sharing moments of her motherhood journey with her fans.

Billy has become a central figure in her life, and Claire often refers to him as her greatest achievement. Her love for her son has shaped much of her perspective, and she has described motherhood as one of the most fulfilling aspects of her life.

Dating and Personal Life After Motherhood

While Claire has kept details of her personal life relatively private in recent years, she has acknowledged her experiences with dating and relationships since becoming a mother.

Focus on Family and Career

Claire has emphasized that her primary focus in recent years has been on balancing her career and being a devoted mother to Billy. She has been selective about the relationships she enters, expressing that she prioritizes her son's well-being and her own happiness above all else.

She has often spoken about the importance of self-love and maintaining a sense of independence while navigating motherhood.

Family Influence and Values

Claire's family background and values have deeply influenced her approach to life and career. Raised in a working-class family in Liverpool, she has often credited her parents and extended family with instilling in her a strong work ethic and a sense of loyalty and love.

Close Family Ties

Claire has a close relationship with her family, particularly with her mother. In interviews, she has spoken about the strong support system her family provided her throughout her career.

Her upbringing in Liverpool played a significant role in shaping her personality, and she has expressed how proud she is of her roots.

Claire has mentioned in interviews that her family has been crucial in supporting her as a mother and as a professional.

Public and Media Scrutiny

As a public figure, Claire Sweeney's relationships have occasionally been subject to media scrutiny. However, she has managed to maintain a sense of dignity and privacy when it comes to her personal life. Despite this, she has openly discussed some of her challenges, including the difficulties of balancing a high-profile career with raising a child.

Media Attention

Over the years, Claire has addressed the pressures that come with being in the public eye and how it affects her relationships. She has worked to maintain boundaries between her public persona and private life, ensuring that her family remains as private and protected as possible.

Reflection on Family and Career

Claire Sweeney's family and relationships have been integral to her personal growth, shaping her values, priorities, and her approach to balancing work with home life. While she is known for her successes in television, theatre, and music, she has always placed a significant emphasis on her role as a mother. Claire's honest reflections on her experiences as a single mother and her relationships have helped humanize her in the eyes of her fans, making her even more relatable.

Her deep connection to her family continues to influence both her personal and professional decisions, ensuring that her family remains at the heart of her narrative as she navigates life and her career in the public spotlight.

Balancing Work and Parenthood

Balancing a demanding career with the responsibilities of parenthood is a challenge that Claire Sweeney has faced with both determination and grace. Throughout her career, she has emphasized the importance of her role as a mother while managing her professional responsibilities, highlighting her ability to juggle the demands of both worlds. Here is a detailed look at how Claire has balanced work and parenthood.

Becoming a Mother: A Turning Point

Claire's life took a significant turn when she became a mother in 2011 with the birth of her son, Billy. This moment was both personally fulfilling and transformative, marking the beginning of a new chapter where her professional life had to be adjusted to accommodate her new responsibilities as a parent.

Motherhood as a Priority:

Following Billy's birth, Claire became very open about her commitment to being an involved and hands-on mother. She has often spoken about how motherhood changed her perspective on life and how she made sure to prioritize her son's needs above everything else.

Claire's experiences with parenthood gave her a renewed sense of purpose, and she described how her son brought her joy, strength, and a deeper understanding of life.

She has spoken candidly about how challenging it can be to balance her demanding career with raising her son, but her commitment to both has always been steadfast.

Adapting Her Career to Fit Parenthood

As a successful actress and performer, Claire has had to adapt her career choices to allow for flexibility and time with her son. She has been selective about the roles and projects she takes on, making sure they align with her family life.

Taking On Flexible Roles:

When it came to choosing her projects post-motherhood, Claire often sought roles that allowed for a balance between her career and being with Billy. This meant taking on television hosting jobs, stage performances, and musical theatre roles that allowed for structured working hours or shorter commitments.

For example, in 2012, Claire starred in the West End production of Hairspray while managing her parental duties. Though demanding, she managed her schedule to ensure she could spend time with Billy while still fulfilling her professional commitments.

Similarly, Claire's participation in reality television shows, such as Celebrity Big Brother and Loose Women, often came with more flexibility in terms of scheduling and time commitments.

Taking Breaks for Family:

Claire has taken breaks from the entertainment industry at times to focus on her family, especially during her son's early years. She has openly discussed stepping back from the limelight to devote herself to motherhood when necessary.

This time away allowed her to give her full attention to Billy during important developmental years, demonstrating her dedication to ensuring that her role as a mother remained her top priority.

Support System and Family Help

Claire's ability to balance her career and family life has been supported by a strong network of family and close friends. Having a reliable support system has been key to managing the demands of both her personal and professional lives.

Family Support:

Claire has always credited her family, particularly her mother, for helping her manage the challenges of motherhood. She has described how her mother played an essential role in supporting her throughout the early years of her son's life, which allowed Claire to pursue her career while ensuring that Billy received the care and attention he needed.

Claire's mother has been a significant part of her support network, and Claire often mentions how much she values her family's help in balancing work and parenthood.

Career Flexibility:

Claire has also been able to lean on her colleagues and industry connections to create a schedule that works for her. She has built relationships in the entertainment industry that have allowed for some flexibility in her roles and commitments.

This has enabled her to maintain a career in the spotlight while also ensuring that she was present for Billy during important milestones.

Maintaining a Positive Outlook on Work-Life Balance

Despite the challenges of balancing work and motherhood, Claire has maintained a positive attitude, often speaking about how rewarding the experience is. She believes that the key to maintaining a work-life balance is being realistic about expectations and learning to prioritize.

Realistic Expectations:

Claire has emphasized the importance of being kind to oneself and recognizing that no one can be perfect at everything. She has acknowledged the challenges of trying to maintain both a successful career and a fulfilling family life, but she encourages other working parents to embrace the messiness of life.

Claire has encouraged other mothers to focus on what works best for them and to not feel pressured by societal expectations of perfection.

Cherishing Family Moments:

Claire has often described how she cherishes the quiet moments she spends with Billy. Despite the pressures of work, she makes sure to carve out time for family activities and ensures that her son feels supported and loved. She has shared how important it is for her to be present for her son, especially as he grows older and becomes more independent.

Public Discussions on Balancing Career and Motherhood

Claire has become a relatable figure for many working mothers, especially those in the public eye. Through her interviews and public appearances, she has openly discussed the complexities of balancing career aspirations with the desire to provide for and nurture her family.

Role Model for Working Mothers:

Claire's honest discussions about her struggles and triumphs in balancing motherhood with a successful career have made her a role model for many working mothers. She serves as an example of how it is possible to navigate a demanding career while maintaining a fulfilling family life.

Her transparency about the sacrifices and rewards of motherhood has allowed her to connect with her audience on a deeper level, particularly with women who face similar challenges.

CHAPTER 8

Philanthropy and Advocacy
Charity Work and Contributions

Throughout her career, Claire Sweeney has not only built a successful career in entertainment but has also been dedicated to giving back to the community through various charitable causes. Her work with charity organizations and her personal contributions to important social issues highlight her commitment to making a positive impact in society. Below is a detailed look at Claire Sweeney's charity work and contributions.

Support for Children's Charities

Claire has been particularly active in supporting children's charities, using her platform to raise awareness and funds for causes that focus on improving the lives of disadvantaged and vulnerable children.

Children in Need

Claire has been a long-time supporter of BBC's Children in Need, a charity telethon that raises money for disadvantaged children in the UK. She has participated in numerous fundraising events and appearances to help raise awareness and support for the charity.

Claire has used her celebrity status to draw attention to the needs of underprivileged children, often taking part in live events or participating in fundraising initiatives.

The Children's Trust

Claire has also worked closely with The Children's Trust, a UK-based charity that supports children with brain injuries and complex health needs. She has participated in fundraising campaigns, charity events, and promotional activities to raise money for the charity's critical work.

Through her involvement, Claire has been instrumental in encouraging public donations and highlighting the importance of rehabilitation and care for children facing serious health challenges.

Breast Cancer Awareness

As a supporter of breast cancer awareness, Claire has actively participated in campaigns that promote early detection, research, and support for those affected by the disease.

Breast Cancer Now

Claire has been involved with Breast Cancer Now, a leading charity dedicated to funding research into breast cancer and providing support for those affected by the disease. She has participated in charity events, marathons, and media campaigns to promote the importance of breast cancer awareness.

Claire's efforts have helped highlight the significance of early screening and research, contributing to the wider conversation about breast cancer prevention and treatment.

Personal Advocacy for Women's Health

As a mother and a woman in the public eye, Claire has used her own platform to raise awareness of women's health issues, particularly breast cancer. Her advocacy has encouraged women to take control of their health by seeking regular check-ups and understanding the importance of self-exams.

Charity Gala Events and Fundraisers

Claire has been involved in organizing and hosting various charity galas and fundraising events, often in collaboration with other celebrities and organizations. These events aim to raise significant funds for vital causes, including those related to health, children's welfare, and education.

Gala Dinners and Auctions

Claire has hosted charity gala dinners and auctions, where high-profile guests and donors come together to raise funds for important causes. These events have raised substantial amounts of money, and Claire's role as a host has helped ensure their success.

Through these events, Claire has raised awareness for causes such as children's healthcare, cancer research, and mental health support.

Support for Mental Health Initiatives

Claire has been vocal about her support for mental health awareness, encouraging open discussions around mental well-being and offering support for those struggling with mental health challenges.

Mind

Claire has supported Mind, a UK-based charity that provides support and information to people experiencing mental health issues. She has participated in campaigns and events to reduce the stigma surrounding mental health and promote understanding and empathy.

Through her involvement with Mind, Claire has advocated for better access to mental health resources and encouraged conversations that normalize mental health struggles.

Raising Awareness for Parents' Mental Health

As a mother, Claire has also spoken about the pressures and challenges of parenting, particularly for single mothers, and the impact this can have on mental health. Her advocacy extends to supporting mental health programs for parents, especially those who are balancing careers with raising children.

Animal Welfare

Claire is a well-known animal lover and has supported various organizations dedicated to animal welfare, including charities that promote the rescue and care of animals.

RSPCA

Claire has worked with the Royal Society for the Prevention of Cruelty to Animals (RSPCA), participating in campaigns to raise awareness of animal cruelty and promote better treatment for animals. She has used her platform to encourage responsible pet ownership and advocate for the welfare of animals in need of care and protection.

Through her work with RSPCA, Claire has helped promote initiatives focused on rescuing abandoned and abused animals.

Personal Donations and Volunteering

Beyond her public charity work, Claire has made personal donations to causes she believes in and has volunteered her time for charitable initiatives. While much of her charity work is done publicly,

Claire has also quietly supported organizations financially, using her resources to make a direct impact.

Personal Financial Contributions

Claire has made personal donations to charities focused on children's health, women's issues, and cancer research. Her financial support helps ensure that these organizations can continue their essential work.

While she is often seen participating in fundraising campaigns, Claire has also quietly made significant contributions behind the scenes, helping sustain charities that depend on ongoing donations to fulfill their missions.

Impact of Claire Sweeney's Charitable Contributions

Claire Sweeney's charity work has had a lasting impact on the causes she supports. By using her public profile to raise awareness and funds, she has contributed significantly to the success of various charity initiatives. Her work with children's charities, breast cancer awareness, mental health, and animal welfare, among others, has helped raise millions of pounds for critical causes.

Her involvement goes beyond simply making public appearances; she is an advocate for change, often speaking passionately about the causes she supports and encouraging others to get involved. Whether through hosting events, participating in media campaigns, or offering personal financial support, Claire has demonstrated a strong commitment to giving back and helping make the world a better place.

Through her charity work, Claire has established herself not just as a public figure but as someone who genuinely cares about improving the lives of others, making her contributions both impactful and inspiring.

Advocacy for Women in the Arts

Claire Sweeney has long been an advocate for the empowerment of women in the arts, using her platform to highlight issues related to gender inequality, representation, and the challenges women face in creative industries. Through her career and personal activism, Claire has consistently championed the importance of supporting women in the arts and ensuring they have opportunities to thrive in all areas of entertainment. Below is a detailed look at Claire Sweeney's advocacy for women in the arts.

Championing Equal Opportunities for Women in the Entertainment Industry

Claire has been outspoken about the importance of providing equal opportunities for women, particularly in theatre, television, and music, where women have historically been underrepresented or pigeonholed into certain roles. She has advocated for breaking down barriers that limit women's creative freedom and professional growth.

Equal Pay and Recognition:

Throughout her career, Claire has expressed concerns over gender disparities in pay and recognition in the arts. She has highlighted the need for fair compensation for women in entertainment, particularly when it comes to acting and singing roles. Claire has used her voice to push for equal treatment and financial remuneration for women working in the arts, ensuring their work is valued equally to their male counterparts.

She has been vocal in advocating for equal recognition of women in both major productions and smaller, often overlooked projects.

Visibility and Opportunities:

Claire has called for greater visibility for women in leadership roles in the arts, including directors, producers, and writers. She believes that when women occupy decision-making positions, the arts community becomes more inclusive, diverse, and reflective of society's experiences.

As a prominent figure in both musical theatre and television, Claire has used her career to shine a light on the struggles women face in getting the recognition and opportunities they deserve.

Encouraging Young Women to Pursue Careers in the Arts

Claire has made it a priority to inspire and mentor young women who are interested in pursuing careers in the arts. Through various interviews, speeches, and outreach programs, she has encouraged young women to follow their passions and not be deterred by societal expectations or limitations.

Mentorship and Guidance:

Claire has shared her own journey as a performer and advocate for women in the arts, offering mentorship to aspiring female artists. She has often spoken about the value of supporting and guiding the next generation of women artists, encouraging them to be bold, creative, and confident in their careers.

Through her public role, she has become a role model for young women seeking careers in theatre, television, and music.

Breaking Stereotypes in Roles:

As an actress, Claire has also been an advocate for breaking stereotypes in the roles women are offered. She has played a diverse range of characters, challenging the typical portrayal of women in mainstream media and pushing for more complex, multidimensional female characters.

Claire believes that showcasing a variety of female experiences in both on-stage and on-screen roles is vital in creating a more inclusive and empowering narrative for women.

Promoting Diversity and Inclusion for Women in the Arts

A core part of Claire's advocacy for women in the arts is the promotion of diversity and inclusion. She has been vocal about the need for the arts to be more inclusive, not just in terms of gender but also race, sexuality, and class.

Inclusive Casting and Representation:

Claire has supported initiatives that aim to increase the representation of women from all walks of life in theatre, television, and film. She has been a strong advocate for casting practices that promote diversity and avoid tokenism.

Claire has consistently spoken out about the importance of ensuring that all women, regardless of their background, have an opportunity to shine in the arts. She supports efforts to create more inclusive casting practices, especially in roles that reflect the diversity of society.

Amplifying Diverse Voices:

Claire's own career has been enriched by her involvement in projects that represent diverse experiences and perspectives. She has used her influence to help amplify voices that are often marginalized in the entertainment industry.

By supporting work that reflects diverse female experiences, Claire has contributed to the broader conversation about the need for representation of women in all their forms, from age and body type to ethnicity and socioeconomic background.

Advocacy Through Media and Public Appearances

In addition to her work on stage and in television, Claire Sweeney has used her media appearances to address issues surrounding women in the arts. She frequently discusses the challenges women face in the entertainment industry, including the pressures of maintaining a public image and the fight for equal treatment in the workplace.

Public Speaking and Interviews:

Through her various public speaking engagements and media interviews, Claire has consistently used her platform to raise awareness of the struggles women face in the arts, particularly around issues like ageism, sexism, and underrepresentation.

She often discusses how women are judged by societal standards of beauty and appearance, and how this affects their opportunities in the entertainment world. By speaking out on these issues, Claire aims to help shift societal views on beauty, talent, and the aging process in the entertainment industry.

Media Representation of Women:

Claire has also addressed the importance of positive media representation for women. She has critiqued the narrow portrayal of women in mainstream media and called for a more diverse and nuanced representation of women's stories, both in front of the camera and behind the scenes.

Work with Female-Focused Organizations and Campaigns

In her personal and professional life, Claire has actively worked with female-focused organizations that support women's rights, empowerment, and leadership in the arts.

Support for Women's Empowerment Initiatives:

Claire has supported organizations that advocate for women's rights and gender equality, particularly in sectors where women's voices have historically been underrepresented. She has used her platform to help raise awareness of these organizations and encourage other women to join in their advocacy efforts.

These efforts help amplify the importance of women supporting women, especially in creative industries where collaboration and shared advocacy can lead to positive change.

CHAPTER 9

Achievements and Recognition
Awards and Honors

Throughout her distinguished career in the entertainment industry, Claire Sweeney has been recognized for her exceptional talent, contributions to the arts, and advocacy for various social causes. Her dedication to her craft and her work in charity, along with her achievements in television, musical theatre, and music, have earned her numerous awards and honors. Below is a comprehensive look at the awards and honors Claire Sweeney has received over the years.

Television and Acting Awards

Claire's performances on television, particularly her role in Brookside, earned her recognition and numerous accolades. Her work in drama, as well as in reality television, helped establish her as a well-known figure in the entertainment industry.

National Television Awards

As a member of the Brookside cast, Claire was part of a show that won the prestigious National Television Award for Best Soap Opera during its run. Though Claire did not win individually, her role in the show contributed to the collective success of the production.

The British Soap Awards

Claire received nominations at the British Soap Awards for her portrayal of Lindsey Corkhill in Brookside. While she didn't win in the categories she was nominated for, her role was widely acclaimed, and her performances helped the show gain recognition from both audiences and critics alike.

Musical Theatre and Performance Recognition

As a prominent figure in musical theatre, Claire Sweeney has been acknowledged for her powerful performances on stage, particularly in productions in the West End.

Olivier Award Nominations

Claire received nominations at the Laurence Olivier Awards, the most prestigious awards in British theatre, for her performances in various musical theatre productions. Her roles in productions like Hairspray and Tell Me on a

Sunday earned her critical acclaim and solidified her reputation as a skilled stage performer.

What's On Stage Awards

Claire received a nomination for Best Actress in a Musical at the What's On Stage Awards, further cementing her status as a leading lady in West End theatre. Her performances have continued to receive positive feedback from both audiences and critics, making her a notable presence in the musical theatre scene.

Music Industry Recognition

While Claire's musical career may not have reached the same level of commercial success as her theatre career, she has been recognized for her musical talents, particularly in her album releases and charity singles.

Chart Success

Claire's debut album Claire Sweeney and her single "You Don't Have to Say You Love Me" achieved commercial success, with her music reaching charts and receiving radio airplay. While her music career was more niche, these successes were important milestones in her journey as an artist.

Charity Recognition

Claire's charity singles, such as those supporting causes like Children in Need, earned her accolades for her commitment to philanthropy through music. Her contributions to charity events and her efforts in raising funds through music were recognized by various charitable organizations and industry figures.

Charity and Community Awards

Claire Sweeney has been recognized for her significant contributions to charity work and her role in raising awareness for various causes. Her dedication to supporting children's charities, breast cancer awareness, and mental health initiatives has been lauded by organizations and foundations.

Celebrity Ambassador and Honorary Recognition

Claire has received honorary awards from several charitable organizations for her involvement in their campaigns. Her role as a celebrity ambassador for organizations like Children in Need and Breast Cancer Now has helped raise millions for critical causes, earning her numerous accolades from these foundations.

The British Red Cross Humanitarian Award

Claire was presented with the British Red Cross Humanitarian Award for her long-standing commitment to supporting humanitarian causes, including her work with vulnerable children, women's health, and mental health initiatives. This award is a testament to Claire's dedication to giving back to her community.

Personal Honors and Recognition

Claire Sweeney's contributions extend beyond her professional career; she has been recognized for her personal qualities as a role model, advocate, and philanthropist.

Pride of Britain Award Nomination

Claire has been nominated for the Pride of Britain Award, a prestigious award that honors individuals who have made a significant impact on society through their charitable work. Claire's efforts to raise awareness of mental health issues and support women's rights in the arts contributed to her nomination for this honor.

Woman of the Year Award

Claire received recognition for her advocacy work in the entertainment industry and for her dedication to charitable causes when she was named Woman of the Year by several organizations, acknowledging her achievements and influence as a role model for women.

Legacy in the Entertainment Industry

Claire Sweeney's legacy in the entertainment industry is marked by her diverse and accomplished career, spanning television, musical theatre, music, and charitable work. Over the years, Claire has solidified herself as one of the UK's most beloved and versatile entertainers, known for her contributions to both the arts and the community. Her legacy is a testament to her resilience, talent, and passion for her craft, as well as her commitment to empowering others. Below is an exploration of her lasting impact and influence on the entertainment industry.

Breaking Boundaries in Television and Soap Opera

One of Claire's most significant contributions to the entertainment industry lies in her pioneering role in the world of soap operas. As one of the standout stars of Brookside, Claire's portrayal of Lindsey Corkhill was pivotal in bringing a fresh and nuanced representation of women to British television. Her character was not only central to the show's plot but also one of the more complex and multidimensional female roles in soap history at the time.

Pioneering Representation of Women in Soap Operas

Claire's role in Brookside helped set a precedent for more diverse and realistic portrayals of women in soap operas. At a time when many female characters in soaps were often one-dimensional or limited to traditional roles, Claire's portrayal broke those molds. Lindsey Corkhill was a character who faced real-world challenges, such as relationship issues, family dynamics, and personal struggles, which resonated with a wide audience.

Impact on the Soap Opera Genre

Claire's work in Brookside not only earned her critical acclaim but also contributed to the genre's evolution. Her character's storylines reflected the increasing complexity of social issues and the ability of soap operas to address sensitive topics with authenticity. Her success in the soap opera world opened doors for future generations of female actors to take on similarly diverse and powerful roles.

Musical Theatre and West End Influence

Claire Sweeney's career in musical theatre is another cornerstone of her legacy. Her stage presence, vocal talent, and dedication to her craft have made her a standout performer in the West End, where she's been involved in some of the most iconic and beloved productions.

Shaping the West End's Musical Landscape

Claire's roles in West End productions such as Hairspray, Tell Me on a Sunday, and Chicago helped to elevate the musical theatre scene in the UK. Her performances were not only highly praised by critics but also drew large audiences, ensuring that these productions remained commercially successful and culturally significant.

Championing Leading Female Roles

Through her work in these high-profile musical productions, Claire has played key roles that helped reframe the way women are represented on stage. Her performances have been central to the narrative of many productions, often taking on complex, empowered female characters who broke from traditional stereotypes. Claire's success in the

West End also highlights the growing importance of women in leading roles in musical theatre, setting a powerful example for young women aspiring to follow in her footsteps.

Influence in Music and Charity through Public Advocacy

Beyond her work on stage and screen, Claire's legacy extends into the music industry and her tireless charity work. Though her music career did not reach the heights of her acting career, Claire's contributions to the charity sector through music have been significant.

Charity Work and Music's Social Impact

Claire's charity singles and her participation in charity events have helped raise millions for causes such as children's health, breast cancer awareness, and mental health. Her efforts to combine her musical talents with her philanthropic passions demonstrated how entertainers can use their platform to create lasting change. Claire's charity work has not only made a tangible impact but also inspired many other entertainers to do the same.

Raising Awareness for Women's Health and Rights

Throughout her career, Claire has been a vocal advocate for women's health, particularly in the areas of breast cancer and mental health. She has helped bring attention to important causes through her music, interviews, and public appearances. By aligning her work with these causes, Claire has cemented herself as a positive role model who encourages others to use their voices to support the greater good.

Cultural Impact and Mentorship

Claire Sweeney's legacy in the entertainment industry also includes her role as a mentor and inspiration to the next generation of performers. Through her advocacy for women in the arts, her involvement in various outreach programs, and her openness about the challenges she faced as a woman in a competitive industry, Claire has paved the way for other women to succeed in the entertainment world.

Mentoring the Next Generation of Talent

As a seasoned performer, Claire has used her experiences to guide and mentor young aspiring artists, particularly women, who are entering the competitive world of musical theatre and television. She has openly shared her journey and the lessons she has learned, offering guidance to the next generation of entertainers. Whether through formal mentorship or simply through public appearances, Claire has been an influential figure for aspiring performers.

Championing Women's Representation in the Arts

Claire's advocacy for increased female representation in the arts has left an indelible mark on the industry. She has consistently called for equal opportunities for women, both on and off stage, and her efforts to push for greater diversity and inclusivity have helped shape the current landscape of British entertainment. By encouraging other women to take leadership roles, Claire has helped ensure that women's voices remain central to the arts.

Continued Influence in the Media

Claire Sweeney's career continues to be a source of inspiration for both her peers and future generations of performers. As a familiar face in the media, Claire's opinions on the entertainment industry, women's rights, and the challenges of balancing family and career carry weight in the public discourse.

Media Contributions and Industry Advocacy

Claire has used her platform to speak out on important issues such as gender equality in the entertainment industry, body image, and the pressures faced by women in the public eye. Her role as an advocate for these issues has helped amplify voices calling for greater equity in the arts. Her continued presence in the media keeps her legacy relevant, ensuring that the issues she cares about continue to be part of the conversation.

CHAPTER 10

Recent Projects
Latest Roles and Performances

Claire Sweeney's most recent professional venture includes participating in the 2024 season of Dancing on Ice, where she is paired with professional skater Colin Grafton. Despite her extensive performance background in musical theatre and television, she is new to ice skating and has shared that her progress so far has been challenging but rewarding. In a candid interview, she mentioned that she has only recently mastered skating backwards, which she considers a major achievement. Her experience in the show is exciting but also daunting, as she navigates the physical demands of ice skating, particularly overcoming her fear of falling.

Additionally, Claire continues to be a presence on Coronation Street, where she plays Cassandra Plummer, the biological mother of Tyrone Dobbs. Her diverse career keeps her actively engaged in both new and familiar roles, balancing her acting career with her ventures into reality television. As she prepares for her debut on the ice, she has also faced speculation that her theatre experience might give her an edge in performance, though she maintains that the challenges of ice skating are unique.

Her latest endeavors highlight her versatility and commitment to exploring new challenges, even as she remains a beloved figure in the entertainment industry.

Continued Relevance in Entertainment

Claire Sweeney's continued relevance in the entertainment industry is evident through her consistent engagement with various media platforms, including television, theatre, and reality shows. Her ability to adapt and remain in the public eye is a testament to her versatility as a performer and her long-lasting appeal.

One of the most notable examples of her sustained relevance is her current role on Dancing on Ice (2024), where she is challenging herself with ice skating, despite her extensive background in acting and musical theatre. Her candidness about being a beginner and facing new challenges has garnered support from fans, and her participation in the show has introduced her to a wider audience, showcasing her willingness to step outside of her comfort zone.

Moreover, her role as Cassandra Plummer on Coronation Street continues to keep her in the spotlight, allowing her to maintain a connection with audiences who have followed her career since her earlier roles in soaps. This role, combined with her previous television appearances and ongoing charity work, ensures that Claire's presence remains strong across different media.

Her involvement in stage productions, such as her notable performances in Chicago and Hairspray, further reinforces her status in the West End, keeping her active in musical theatre. This dual presence in television and theatre underlines her sustained relevance in both traditional and contemporary entertainment spaces.

By diversifying her roles and embracing new formats, Claire Sweeney continues to stay relevant, not just as an entertainer, but as a figure who bridges multiple generations of viewers.

Conclusion

Reflection on Her Career

Claire Sweeney's career offers a rich tapestry of achievements across television, theatre, and music, marking her as a versatile and enduring figure in the entertainment industry. Reflecting on her career reveals a remarkable ability to evolve while remaining true to her roots, demonstrating both resilience and a willingness to embrace new challenges.

Television Legacy

Sweeney's role in Brookside was a career-defining moment, launching her into the spotlight and cementing her place in British television history. As Lindsey Corkhill, she captured the complexities of a strong yet flawed character, helping to shape the portrayal of women in soap operas. Even as she moved on from the series, she returned to television in various other capacities, from hosting to participating in reality shows like Dancing on Ice. This adaptability has kept her relevant across generations, appealing to both new and longtime fans.

Stage Performances

Sweeney's work in musical theatre, particularly in Chicago and Hairspray, demonstrates her incredible stage presence and vocal talent. These roles not only showcased her acting chops but also her capacity to command the stage in some of the West End's most iconic productions. By balancing her presence in both television and theatre, Claire has carved out a unique position for herself as an entertainer who thrives in various formats.

Musical and Charitable Contributions

Though her music career didn't achieve mainstream commercial success, her charity singles and involvement in numerous philanthropic causes illustrate her commitment to using her platform for good. This part of her career highlights her empathy and the broader impact she seeks to have, beyond entertainment.

Continued Evolution and Public Persona

Claire's continued presence in reality shows like Dancing on Ice and her role in Coronation Street reflect a constant reinvention of herself, maintaining her relevance in a highly competitive industry. She is not afraid to step outside of her comfort zone, which is a key element in her ongoing success.

Influence on the Entertainment World

Claire Sweeney has had a lasting influence on the entertainment world, with her multifaceted career spanning television, theatre, music, and charity work. Her ability to evolve and remain relevant in the industry is a testament to her versatility and broad appeal, making her an influential figure in British entertainment.

1. Pioneering Roles and Representation

One of Sweeney's most significant contributions to the entertainment world was her role in Brookside, where she portrayed Lindsey Corkhill. As one of the central characters in the show, she helped break traditional gender norms in soap operas by portraying a strong yet vulnerable female character. This representation of complex women in television helped shape future storylines for female characters in British soaps.

2. Impact on Musical Theatre

Sweeney's success on the West End also contributed to the development and popularity of British musical theatre. Through her performances in productions like Chicago and Hairspray, she showcased her strong vocal and performance abilities, making musical theatre more accessible to a broader audience. Her presence in the West End helped reaffirm the significance of musical theatre in contemporary British entertainment, and her ability to juggle both television and stage performances set a powerful example for aspiring performers.

3. Influence in Reality Television

Her participation in shows like Dancing on Ice and her previous stint in Celebrity Big Brother has allowed her to reach a new generation of viewers. By stepping into the reality television arena, Claire showed that even seasoned performers could thrive in formats that are typically associated with fresh faces. This willingness to embrace new genres has solidified her role as a versatile entertainer.

4. Advocacy and Charitable Influence

Sweeney's involvement in charity work also highlights her influence beyond entertainment. Through her music, public appearances, and charity singles, she has used her platform to raise awareness for various causes, including breast cancer awareness and children's health. Her advocacy work has not only impacted those in need but has also inspired other entertainers to use their platforms for social good.

Printed in Dunstable, United Kingdom

64701622R00067